The First Christmas

A PLAY & LEARN BOOK

Edited by Jill C. Lafferty
Illustrations by Peter Grosshauser

SPARK
HOUSE
FAMILY

The First Christmas

You might already know a lot about the first Christmas. You might know that it's the night Jesus was born in a stable in Bethlehem. You might know about the shepherds and the angels and the wise men who brought gifts. But did you know that people were talking about Jesus hundreds of years before he was born?

The Old Testament tells us of God's promise to send a Savior who would live among the people and bring peace and healing to the whole world. God's people wondered what kind of great leader the Savior would be. Imagine what a surprise it was for the Savior to arrive as a tiny baby and not a powerful ruler!

In this Play and Learn book, you'll find a collection of Bible stories about the promises God made and how God kept those promises by giving us the gift of Jesus, God's Son. Some people, like Mary, were shocked by the news of this baby. Others, like Herod, were angry and afraid. And others, like Simeon and Anna, understood that Jesus was the promised Savior, the one God had sent to bring peace.

As you and your family explore your Play and Learn book, see if you can find a story where someone:

• Tells others about God's promise of a Savior
• Believes Jesus is the promised Savior
• Is surprised or excited about the news of Jesus' birth

Each story in this Play and Learn book gives you a verse to remember, some fun activities to try, and ideas for celebrating the gift of Jesus. So jump in and discover more about the first Christmas!

Published by Sparkhouse Family
510 Marquette Avenue
Minneapolis, MN 55402
sparkhouse.org

© 2016 Sparkhouse Family

All rights reserved.

The First Christmas
Play and Learn Book
First edition published 2016

Printed in United States
21 20 19 18 17 16   1 2 3 4 5 6 7 8
9781506417639

Edited by Jill C. Lafferty
Cover design by Tory Herman
Cover illustration by Peter Grosshauser
Interior designed by Tory Herman
Interior photographs provided by
iStock and Thinkstock
Illustrations by Peter Grosshauser

All Bible quotations are from THE HOLY
BIBLE, NEW INTERNATIONAL VERSION®,
NIV®. Copyright © 1973, 1978, 1984, 2011
by Biblica, Inc.® Used by permission
of Zondervan. All rights reserved
worldwide. www.zondervan.com. The
"NIV" and "New International Version"
are trademarks registered in the United
States Patent and Trademark Office by
Biblica, Inc.™

V63474; 9781506417639; JUN2016

Table of Contents

How to Use Your Spark Story Bible Play and Learn Book

Each section in this Play and Learn book includes a short story from the Bible, followed by all kinds of engaging ways to think about the theme of the story. Look for these activities in every story.

The Story
Start here. You'll get a summary of the Bible story you'll explore on the pages to come.

A Prayer to Share
Cut out these prayers to help you talk to God about what you've learned.

BE NEAR US
Lord Jesus.
Amen.

s Is Born

d kept the promise of Jesus!

God promised Mary and Joseph a special baby. Now it was time for the baby to be born. But Mary and Joseph were on a trip to Bethlehem! The only place with room for them to stay was a little stable. That's where Jesus was born. Angels announced the birth to shepherds, and everyone rejoiced and praised Jesus!

HOW DO YOU REJOICE?
WHO REJOICED THE
DAY YOU WERE BORN?

Squiggles feels eager.
He wants to see baby Jesus.

How does
YOUR face
look when you
feel eager?

Conversation Starters
Talk about these questions as a family. Make sure everyone gets a chance to share their thoughts.

Explore with Squiggles
This expressive little caterpillar responds to each story with a specific emotion and invites children to do the same.

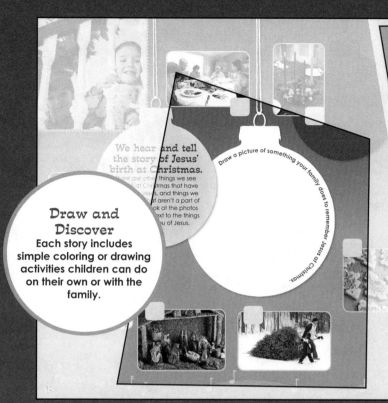

In the Bible AND In Our World!

Mary and Joseph lived in Nazareth, but they traveled to Bethlehem, the home of Joseph's family, for a census. (A census counts all of the people living in an area.) The distance Mary and Joseph traveled from Nazareth to Bethlehem is about 70 miles. Today, Bethlehem is a small city near Jerusalem. The majority of people who live there are Muslim, but it's home to one of the world's oldest Christian communities too.

The Holy Land today

Church of the Nativity in Bethlehem

We hear and tell the story of Jesus' birth at Christmas.

There are other things we see at Christmas that have to do with Jesus, and things we do that aren't a part of it. Look at the photos and next to the things that remind you of Jesus.

Draw a picture of something your family does to remember Jesus at Christmas.

Draw and Discover
Each story includes simple coloring or drawing activities children can do on their own or with the family.

In Our World
Find out more about how the themes of the stories show up in our lives today.

Make Time for Pretend Fun!
Pretend a doll or action figure is baby Jesus. Cuddle baby Jesus close and sing "Away in a Manger!" Give the baby a kiss on the forehead. How else would you take care of baby Jesus? Remember that Jesus loves you!

42   43

Do You Know?

An Old Testament prophet shared a promise from God that Jesus would be born in Bethlehem. Answer these questions about Jesus. Use each answer to find out the name of that prophet. Find out!

1. Jesus' mother's name is _____

2. Jesus was born in a manger because there was no _____

3. Bethlehem is also called the _____ of David.

4. Jesus' birth was announced by _____

5. The angels sang "Glory to God in the highest _____"

The prophet who said Jesus would be born in Bethlehem was _____

A Puzzle to Solve
Word games, mazes, connect-the-dots, and other puzzles and games help you explore the themes of the story.

A Verse to Learn
Say these verses together or try to memorize them as a family.

Glory to God in the highest heaven, and on earth peace to those on whom his favor rests.
Luke 2:14

This verse is a song that the angels in the sky sang to the shepherds in the field. Try singing the verse together to a familiar tune or one you make up. When you have it down, add real or pretend instruments to the song too.

Look It Up!
Read the whole story for yourselves from your Bible or *Spark Story Bible.*

There's MORE to this story!
Read the WHOLE story in your Bible together! You can find it in the 3rd New Testament book:

Luke 2:1-20

In the Spark Story Bible, look for Jesus Is Born on pages 198-203.

Make Time for Los Posadas Fun
In Mexico, Christians celebrate Christmas by re-enacting Joseph and Mary's search for a place to stay. The nine-day celebration, ending the day before Christmas, is called *Los Posadas.* (*Posada* is Spanish for "lodging.") You can celebrate this in your home: Two people pretend to be Mary and Joseph. Everyone else goes into different rooms and closes the door. "Mary" and "Joseph" knock on doors and ask if they can stay there. Afterward, throw a fiesta (party) to celebrate the good news of Jesus' birth.

Family Fun!
Put your learning into action with these family activity ideas.

44   45

God Will Bring Peace

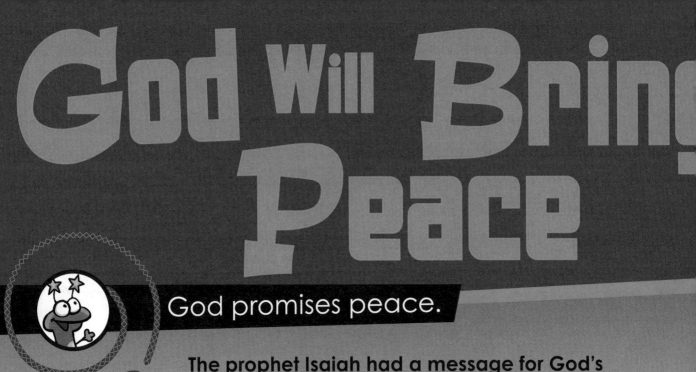

God promises peace.

The prophet Isaiah had a message for God's people. "Listen to my good news!" he said. "God loves us. God will send us a great teacher who will show us how to live in peace." **We believe that teacher is Jesus!**

Cut out this prayer, say the prayer together, then put it in an envelope. Deliver the envelope to someone else to help share the good news of Jesus.

THANK YOU, God, for sending Jesus to teach us about peace. Amen.

✂

WHAT DO YOU THINK PEACE MEANS?

WHY ARE PROMISES HARD TO KEEP SOMETIMES?

Squiggles feels trusting. He believes that God will bring peace!

How does **YOUR** face look when you feel trusting?

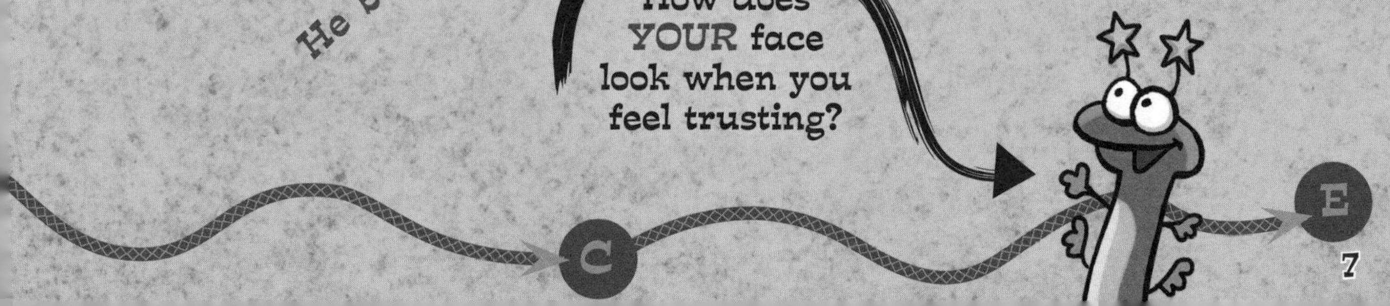

C

E

God's people had to wait a long time for Jesus.

Waiting is hard. Look at the photos. What do you think the kids are waiting for in each photo? Write a ✓ on the photos that show ways you've waited. In the box, write a way you can wait peacefully.

I can wait peacefully by . . .

There's MORE to this story!

Read the WHOLE story in your Bible together! You can find it in the book named after the prophet with God's good news!

Isaiah 2:1-5

Isaiah told everyone that God would bring peace. All around the world, people pray for peace. Learn to say **PEACE** in other languages.

Russian: mir
Spanish: paz
Mandarin Chinese: hépíng (HUA-peen)
Hebrew: shalom (shah-LOHM)
Swedish: fred (FREE-ed)
Arabic: salaam (sah-LEM)
Swahili: amani (ah-MAH-nee)

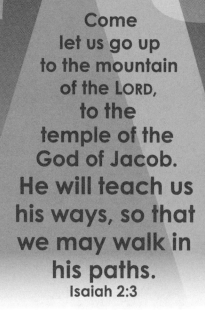

Come let us go up to the mountain of the LORD, to the temple of the God of Jacob. He will teach us his ways, so that we may walk in his paths.
Isaiah 2:3

Put on a backpack and pretend you are climbing a big mountain. Say this verse together while you take steps up the "mountain," one word per step. Repeat the verse until you get to the top. Lift your knees higher and higher.

Are you there yet?

Make Time for More Fun!

God makes and keeps lots of promises. What can you promise to do this week that would help make your home more peaceful? You could promise to keep your room clean, play with your brother, pick up your toys, do your homework without being asked, or clean up after supper. Make a promise and then keep it!

God's Peace World

We can live in peace.

God gave Isaiah a message to share. A time would come when wolves and lambs will play together. Baby goats will nap safely next to leopards. Even the shy calf and the mighty lion will be friends. A little child will show everyone how to live in peace and love one another. Isaiah's message gave people hope.

★ WHAT MAKES IT HARD TO LIVE PEACEFULLY WITH OTHERS?

WHEN HAVE YOU FELT PEACE?

Cut out this prayer and tape it to a map or globe. Point to the places where there is fighting or where people are hurting. Remember these places as you say the prayer together.

GOD, let us show the world your peace. Bring peace everywhere. Amen.

Squiggles feels hopeful. Peace is possible with God's help!

How does YOUR face look when you feel hopeful?

RINI . . . PEACE . . . SHALOM . . . SHANTI . . . FRIEDEN . . . PACEM . . . PAX . . . AMANI .

11

There's MORE to this stor

Read the WHOLE story in your Bible togeth
You can find it the middle of the Bible:

Isaiah 11:1-10

In the Spark Story Bible, look for
God's Peaceful World on pages 166-169.

The **wolf** will live with the **lamb**, the leopard
will lie down with the goat, the calf and the lion and
the yearling together; and a little child will lead them.

Isaiah 11:6

This verse talks about animals living in peace, but in God's peaceful world people
can get along too! Who are some people who have trouble getting along? Say
this verse together, then say it a second time, replacing the animals with names of
people your family hopes will live in peace.

"_____ will live with _____ , _____ will

down with _____ , _____ and _____ ar

_____ together; and a little child will lead them."

Make Time fo
More Fun!

Gather animal toys and
set up your own family
zoo. Work together to pla
where each animal will liv
Which animals should be
separated? Which animal
could you put together
safely? If your zoo was in th
peaceful world described
by Isaiah, how would your
zoo's design change?

In the animal world, a **predator** eats other animals.
Animals that get eaten are called **prey**.

Match each predator with its prey. With another color, scribble over the lines. How would these animals act in God's peaceful world? How could these animals play together peacefully?

What does this word mean to you?

PEACE

COLOR THIS WORD. God's peace is more than just not fighting—it means living God's way and loving each other. It's hard to completely understand God's peace, but Isaiah writes about how peace will feel in God's kingdom.

RINI . . . PEACE . . . SHALOM . . . SHANTI . . . FRIEDEN . . . PACEM . . . PAX . . . AMANI . . . VREDE . . . SALAM . . . PE . . . IRINI . . . HE PING . . . PAIX

A Child Called Immanuel

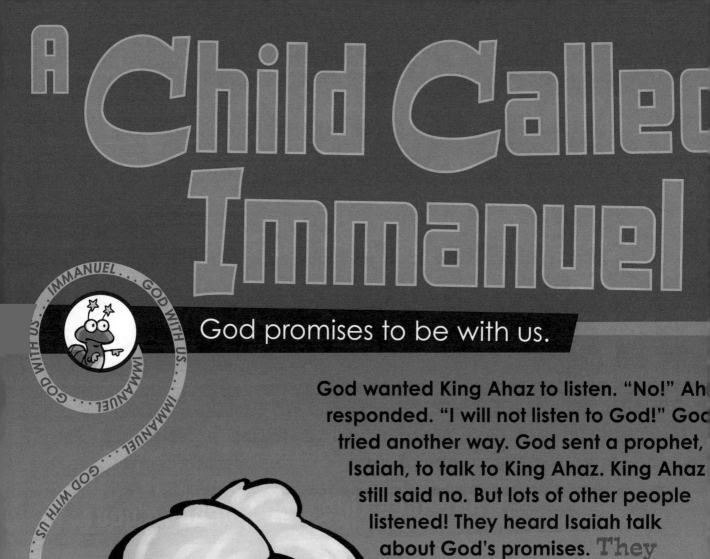

God promises to be with us.

God wanted King Ahaz to listen. "No!" Ahaz responded. "I will not listen to God!" God tried another way. God sent a prophet, Isaiah, to talk to King Ahaz. King Ahaz still said no. But lots of other people listened! They heard Isaiah talk about God's promises. They heard that God promised a Son named Immanuel.

Squigg
Why we

Cut out this prayer and tape it to an alarm clock or timer. Listen for the alarm. Say the prayer together when the alarm goes off.

GOD, help us listen to you and say YES to you. Amen.

WHEN DO YOU SAY NO? WHAT HELPS YOU SAY YES?

Immanuel means "God with us."

...Is confused.
...g Ahaz listen to God?

...w does YOUR
...e look when
...u feel confused?

😦 😊

😦 😊

Isaiah told King Ahaz that God would send a sign— a baby named Immanuel.

Signs can tell us good news or bad news. Look at the photos. If you think the photo shows a good sign, circle the smiley face. If you think the photo shows a bad or sad sign, circle the sad face.

😦 😊

😦 😊

😦 😊

😦 😊

There's MORE to this story!
Read the WHOLE story in your Bible together!
You can find it in the prophets section of the Old Testament:

Isaiah 7:10-17

In the Spark Story Bible, look for
A Child Called Immanuel on pages 162-165.

Immanuel
is pronounced
ih-MAN-yoo-ehl.

EL . . . GO . . . IMMANUEL . . . GOD WITH US . . . IMM . . . GOD WITH US . . . IMMANUEL . . .

Do You Know? Answers: 1. David; 2. Herod; 3. Jesus.

Do You Know?

There are lots of kings in the Bible. Sometimes kings listened to God, and sometimes they didn't. Use your Bible to learn more about some of these kings.

1. I was a shepherd boy when I found out I would be king. Jesus was born from my family line. Who am I? *(See 1 Samuel 1:16-17.)*

_____

2. I was afraid of baby Jesus, so I tried to trick the wise men into telling me where he was. Who am I? *(See Matthew 2:1-12.)*

_____

3. I am a different kind of king. I don't wear a crown. My power is about loving God. Who am I? *(See Matthew 27:11-14.)*

_____

Make Time for More Fun!

King Ahaz did not want to listen to God or God's prophet, Isaiah. Play a game to show how well you can listen. Take turns closing your eyes while someone makes a sound (knocking on the floor, rubbing hands together, playing a note on an instrument, and so on). See if you can identify all the sounds using only your ears.

Therefore the Lord himself will give you a sign: The virgin will conceive and give birth to a son, and will call him **Immanuel.**
Isaiah 7:14

IMMANUEL is a special name we use for Jesus. What special names or nicknames do you call each other in your family? Say the verse together, and then talk about the special names you call each other. Draw a picture of your family, and write a special name next to each person.

A Good Ruler

God remembers us!

After King David died, some bad kings ruled God's people, the Israelites. Life was hard. God called a man named Jeremiah to give God's people hope. "God hasn't forgotten you," Jeremiah told the Israelites. "And God will send a good ruler soon." The Israelites were overjoyed. God remembered them!

Squiggles feels sad! Life was hard for the Israelites.

How does YOUR face look when you feel sad?

WHO ALWAYS REMEMBERS YOU? WHO WILL YOU NEVER FORGET?

Cut out this prayer and attach yarn or string so that you can hang the prayer on a doorknob. Say the prayer anytime you go through the door.

GOD, Thanks for always remembering us! Amen.

GOd remembers us in hard times.

God remembers us in happy and sad and mad and funny times too. Talk about the feelings of the people in the pictures. Make a face like each person. Circle a picture that shows a feeling you had today. God was with you!

"The days are coming," declares the LORD, "when I will fulfill the good promise I made to the people of Israel and Judah."

Jeremiah 33:14

God made a promise to the people of Israel and Judah. Have you ever made a pinky promise? Lock your pinky with a partner and say the verse together.

There's MORE to this story!

Read the WHOLE story in your Bible together! You can find it in the prophets section of the Old Testament:

Jeremiah 33:14-17

Do You Know?

God made a promise and kept it. What was the promise? How was the promise fulfilled? Unscramble the letters to complete the sentences!

God promised to send a good

_____ _____ _____ _____ _____ _____

to save the world.

His name is

_____ _____ _____ _____ _____ !

Make Time for More Fun!

God remembered the Israelites. How much can YOU remember? Play a memory game and find out! Sit in a circle with your family or friends. Say, "I want a king who's a *good* king." The next person adds something else (". . . a good king and a *mighty* king"). Each person adds another description until the list is too hard to remember!

A Ruler from Bethlehem

Jesus leads us.

The people of Bethlehem felt scared and hopeless. Then God's messenger, Micah, shared good news: the greatest leader the world had even seen would be born in Bethlehem! This leader would care for all people, especially those who need extra help. **The message gave the people hope!**

Squiggles feels hopeful whe hearing Micah's good new

How does **YOUR** face look when you feel hopeful?

Cut out this prayer and tape it to your television or computer. After reading or watching the news, pray together for your leaders.

GOD, help leaders in our country, church, school, workplace, neighborhood, and home to make good choices. Amen.

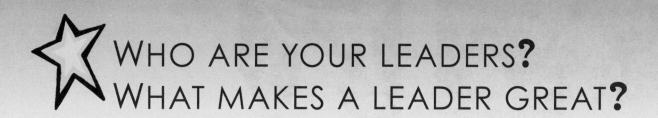

WHO ARE YOUR LEADERS?
WHAT MAKES A LEADER GREAT?

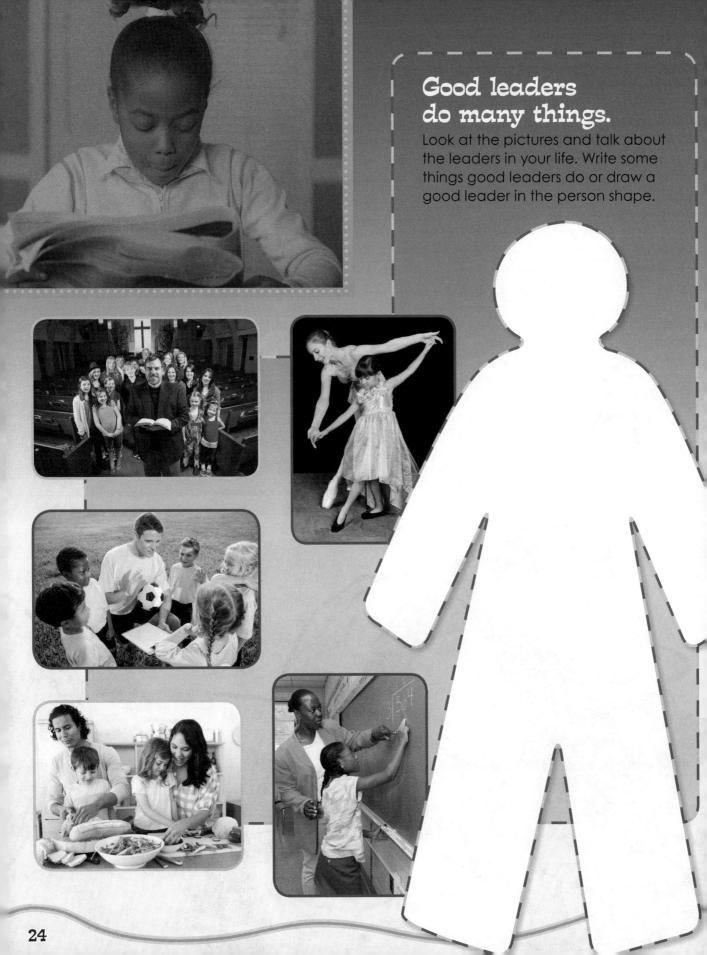

Good leaders do many things.

Look at the pictures and talk about the leaders in your life. Write some things good leaders do or draw a good leader in the person shape.

In the Bible AND In Our World!

Micah's message from God promised that the greatest ruler ever would be born in Bethlehem. The town of Bethlehem still exists today, and many Christian pilgrims (religious travelers) journey to Bethlehem to see the Church of the Nativity. This church was built over the cave where many believe Jesus was born.

Make Time for Singing Fun!

Sing Christmas carols that mention Bethlehem:
"O Little Town of Bethlehem,"
"Hark! The Herald Angels Sing,"
"O Come, All Ye Faithful."
What do these songs say about Bethlehem? About God and Jesus? Sing some of these songs together and go caroling!

Do You Know?

What do you know about Bethlehem and the leaders who were born there? Test your knowledge:

1. What does Bethlehem mean?

 _____ of _____

2. What two great rulers were born in Bethlehem?

 _____ and _____

(See 1 Samuel 16:4-13 and Luke 2:4-7)

3. David played the _____ (rhymes with *fire*)

and was handy with a _____.

4. Jesus said, "I am the _____ of life."

(John 6:35)

There's MORE to this story!

Read the WHOLE story in your Bible together! You can find it near the end of the Old Testament:

Micah 5:2-5

In the Spark Story Bible, look for *A Ruler from Bethlehem* on pages 184-185.

Micah is pronounced **MY-kuh.**

Make Time for Game Fun!

Play Follow the Leader with family and friends in your home, **at the park, on the beach,** or wherever **you have enough space.**

Let different people take turns being the leader. Each time you switch leaders, pause to chat about what it means to be a leader and what good leaders do. How can your family follow Jesus, the greatest leader ever, more closely?

He will stand and shepherd his flock in the strength of the LORD, in the majesty of the name of the LORD his God. And they will live securely, for then his greatness will reach to the ends of the earth.
Micah 5:4

Take turns having one person stand straight and shout out the words in **yellow**, with everyone else kneeling and saying in a calm voice the words in **blue**.

God promised a Son named Jesus.

An angel gave a young woman named Mary some surprising news. "You will have a baby named Jesus," the angel said. "A baby?" Mary wondered. Mary was engaged to a man named Joseph, but they weren't married yet. The angel went to see Joseph too. "Mary will have a baby named Jesus," the angel said. "A baby?" Joseph wondered. Mary and Joseph trusted God.

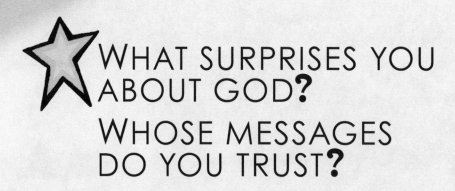

WHAT SURPRISES YOU ABOUT GOD?

WHOSE MESSAGES DO YOU TRUST?

Cut out this prayer and use it as a bookmark in your family Bible to help you find your favorite story about Jesus. Say the prayer when you use your Bible. Use the back to write down surprising things you learn about God.

THANK YOU, God, for sending Jesus. Amen.

Squiggles feels shocked. The angel is so bright!

How does YOUR face look when you feel shocked?

Surprising things I've learned about God:

_____
_____
_____
_____
_____
_____
_____
_____
_____
_____

Mary and Joseph felt a lot of different emotions when they heard the angel's news: they were surprised, sad, confused, and joyful.

Look at the photos. Draw a line or trace a path from each photo to the child in the middle who shows the way you'd feel about what's happening in the photo.

SAD HAPPY SURPRISED

There's MORE to this story!
Read the WHOLE story in your Bible together! You can find it in two Gospel books:
Matthew 1:18-25; Luke 1:26-38
In the Spark Story Bible, look for *Angels Visit* on pages 186-191.

Make Time for More Helping Fun

Do you know a family getting ready for a new baby? Surprise them with a gift. Work together to make and freeze some healthy soup for the new baby's family to eat when they are busy and tired after the baby is born.

What does this word mean to you?

HOLY

COLOR THIS WORD. The angel told Mary that her child would be holy. *Holy* describes people or things that are special for God.

The angel said to her, "Do not be afraid, Mary; you have found favor with God."

Luke 1:30

It's normal to be afraid of things in the world, but we can remember that God is always with us. Gather together and read the verse out loud. Talk about times when you were afraid of something. Say the words, "Do not be afraid," to each other in the same tender way the angel said the words to Mary.

Mary Visits Elizabeth

We watch for God's surprises.

Mary was bursting with excitement! She had to tell someone about the baby she would give birth to. She could visit her cousin Elizabeth! Elizabeth was pregnant too. Elizabeth's baby jumped for joy inside her at the sound of Mary's voice! **God kept promises to Mary and Elizabeth.**

Squiggles feels surprised.
God is doing big things!

How does **YOUR** face look
when you feel surprised?

Surprise! Surprise! Surprise! Surprise! Surprise!

**GOD, make us ready
for whatever surprises
you have in store
for us. Amen.**

Surprise!   Surprise!   Surprise!

Cut out this prayer and take
turns hiding it in places where
you know someone will find
it. Whoever finds it gets to say
the prayer and hide it again.

WHAT
SURPRISES
YOU?

WHAT DO
YOU LIKE
OR NOT
LIKE ABOUT
SURPRISES?

There's MORE to this story!

Read the WHOLE story in your Bible together! You can find it in the 3rd book in the New Testament:

Luke 1:39-58

In the Spark Story Bible, look for the New Testament story Mary Visits Elizabeth on pages 192-197.

Mary and Elizabeth were both getting ready for babies.
What do babies need? Write or draw things that a baby needs.

Clothing

Toys or books

Food

Safety

Do you know? Answers: 1. John, 2. He prepared people for the coming of Jesus

When Elizabeth heard Mary's greeting, the baby leaped in her womb, and Elizabeth was filled with the Holy Spirit.

Luke 1:41

Take turns reading this passage while everyone jumps up and down!

Make Time for More Fun!

As a family, make a list of all the babies you know who have been born in the last year. Together, write a prayer for these babies and pray for them.

Do You Know?

Who is the baby who leaped in Elizabeth's womb? Like Jesus, this baby would have a special job to do for God.

1. What was his name? (See Luke 1:59-63.)

_____

2. What special job did he have? (See Matthew 3:1-6.)

_____

_____

Zechariah

We are friends of Jesus!

Elizabeth and her husband, Zechariah, took their baby to the temple for his naming ceremony. They chose the name John. Zechariah sang for joy about how Jesus would come to help everyone and how John would be a friend of Jesus. John would help people get ready for Jesus.

WHO ARE YOUR FRIENDS?
HOW DO FRIENDS HELP EACH OTHER?

Squiggles feels relieved that Jesus would have a friend to help him.

How does YOUR face look when you feel relieved?

Zechariah is pronounced **zeh-kuh-RYE-uh.**

Cut out this prayer and write the names of friends on the back. Be sure to include Jesus! At mealtime or bedtime, take turns saying the prayer.

THANK YOU, God, for my friend _____. Help me to be a good friend to [him/her]. Amen.

Friends do lots of stuff together.

What are the friends in these pictures doing? If you've done any of these things with a friend, write the name of your friend or make a checkmark on that photo. How is Jesus your friend?

And you, my child, will be called a prophet of the Most High; for you w

Make Time for More Fun!

Zechariah sang about John and Jesus. Both babies' names begin with the letter J! Take a walk around your home or neighborhood naming things in God's creation that begin with J. Every time you add a new thing, repeat the entire list. If your list gets too long to remember, start again with a different letter.

 Our Friends

Do You Know?

Zechariah sang about what John would do when he grew up. Complete this crossword based on Luke 1:68-79.

Across

1. Zechariah blessed the God of _____. (v. 68)
2. John would be a _____ of the Most High. (v. 76)
3. God remembered the _____ (promise) with Israel. (v. 72)

Down

4. God's people would be guided to the path of _____. (v. 79)
5. The Savior would be from the house of _____. (v. 69)
6. God made the promise with _____. (v. 73)

... on before the Lord to prepare the way for him.
Luke 1:76

Get paper, markers, scissors, and tape. Prepare 8 footprints by drawing around family members' feet. Write a word or phrase of the verse on each footprint. Cut out the footprints and tape them to the floor to form a path. Take turns stepping on each footprint while you say the verse. Walk faster each time!

There's MORE to this story!

Read the WHOLE story in your Bible together! You can find it in the Gospel that was written by a doctor: **Luke 1:68-79**

Jesus Is Born

God kept the promise of Jesus!

God promised Mary and Joseph a special baby. Now it was time for the baby to be born. But Mary and Joseph were on a trip to Bethlehem! The only place with room for them to stay was a little stable. That's where Jesus was born. Angels announced the birth to shepherds, and everyone rejoiced and praised Jesus!

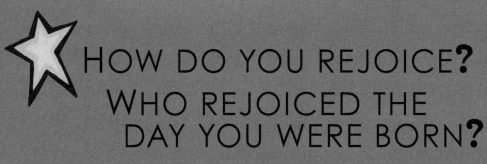

HOW DO YOU REJOICE? WHO REJOICED THE DAY YOU WERE BORN?

Cut out this prayer and put it under a pillow. Pray the prayer together before you go to sleep.

BE NEAR US Lord Jesus. Amen.

Squiggles feels eager. He wants to see baby Jesus.

How does **YOUR** face look when you feel eager?

We hear and tell the story of Jesus' birth at Christmas.

There are other things we see and do at Christmas that have to do with Jesus, and things we see and do that aren't a part of Jesus' story. Look at the photos and put a star next to the things that remind you of Jesus.

Draw a picture of something your family does at Christmas.

In the Bible AND In Our World!

Mary and Joseph lived in Nazareth, but they traveled to Bethlehem, the home of Joseph's family, for a census. (A census counts all of the people living in an area.) The distance Mary and Joseph traveled from Nazareth to Bethlehem is about 70 miles. Today, Bethlehem is a small city near Jerusalem. The majority of people who live there are Muslim, but it's home to one of the world's oldest Christian communities too.

Har Meron ▲

Nazareth

Jordan River

Jerusalem ★
Bethlehem ●

Dead Sea

ISRAEL

Church of the Nativity in Bethlehem

Make Time for Pretend Fun!

Pretend a doll or action figure is baby Jesus. Cuddle baby Jesus close and sing "Away in a Manger." Give the baby a kiss on the forehead. How else would you take care of baby Jesus? Remember that Jesus loves you!

Do You Know?

An Old Testament prophet shared a promise from God that a savior (Jesus!) would be born in Bethlehem. Answer these questions about Jesus, and use the first letter of each answer to find out the name of that prophet. Find all the answers in Luke 2:1-20.

1. Jesus' mother's name is _____.

2. Jesus was born in a manger because there was no _____.

3. Bethlehem is also called the _____ of David.

4. Jesus' birth was announced by _____.

5. The angels sang "Glory to God in the highest _____."

The prophet who said Jesus would be born in Bethlehem was

□ □ □ □ □ .

There's MORE to this story!

Read the WHOLE story in your Bible together! You can find it in the 3rd New Testament book:

Luke 2:1-20

In the Spark Story Bible, look for *Jesus Is Born* on pages 198-203.

Glory to God in the highest heaven, and on earth peace to those on whom his favor rests.
Luke 2:14

This verse is a song that the angels in the sky sang to the shepherds in the field. Try singing the verse together to a familiar tune or one you make up. When you have it down, add real or pretend instruments to the song too.

Make Time for Los Posadas Fun

In Mexico, Christians celebrate Christmas by re-enacting Joseph and Mary's search for a place to say. The nine-day celebration, ending the day before Christmas, is called *Los Posadas.* (*Posada* is Spanish for "lodging.") You can celebrate this in your home: Two people pretend to be Mary and Joseph. Everyone else goes into different rooms and closes the door. "Mary" and "Joseph" knock on doors and ask if they can stay there. Afterward, throw a fiesta (party) to celebrate the good news of Jesus' birth.

Do You Know? Answers: 1. Mary; 2. guest room; 3. town; 4. angels; 5. heaven. The prophet's name is MICAH.

45

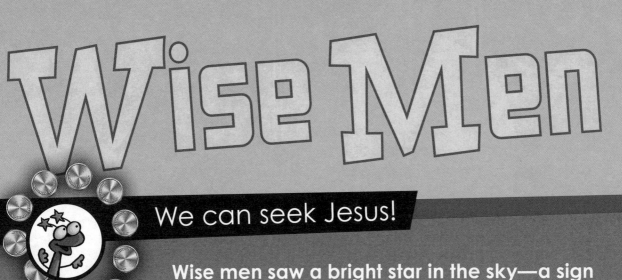

Wise Men

We can seek Jesus!

Wise men saw a bright star in the sky—a sign from God to find baby Jesus! On the way, they asked King Herod where Jesus might be. Herod tried to trick the men so that he could hurt Jesus. The wise men found Jesus, gave him gifts, and then went home on a different road to avoid Herod.

Squiggles feels curious! Where will the star take them?

How does YOUR face look when you feel curious?

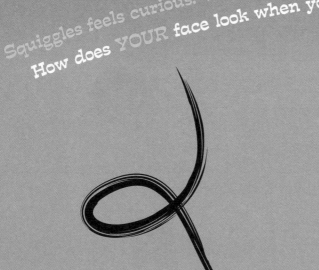

GOD, thank you for shining your light into this world! Amen.

Cut out this prayer and tape it in the upper corner of a window where you can see the night sky. Pray it together before going to bed each night.

 WHAT DOES IT MEAN TO BE WISE? WHAT GIFT WOULD YOU GIVE JESUS?

There's MORE to this story!

Read the WHOLE story in your Bible together! You can find it in the 1st book of the New Testament:

Matthew 2:1-12

In the Spark Story Bible, look for the New Testament story titled Wise Men on pages 204-209.

We don't need a star to seek Jesus.

Draw a ⭐ on photos that show ways you seek Jesus.

In the big star, write a way your family can seek Jesus this week.

Our family can seek Jesus this week by . . .

Do You Know?

After the wise men went home, King Herod tried to find another way to find and hurt Jesus. An angel warned Joseph to hide his family. Where did they go? Circle every 3rd letter and write the letters in order in the blanks to find out! *(Hint: See Matthew 2:13-15.)*

X U E B M G O L Y V W P I W T C L

_ _ _ _ _ _ _

Where is the one who has been born king of the Jews? We saw his star when it rose and have come to worship him.

Matthew 2:2

Go outside in the evening together and point at the sky while reading this verse out loud!

Make Time for More Fun!

Use a telescope, go on the Internet, or use a star app to learn about the night sky together as a family. What constellations are visible at this time of year? Keep a list of the ones you've seen. Which ones show up in other seasons? What's the coolest thing you've ever seen in the sky?

Escape to Egypt

God keeps us safe.

King Herod didn't like baby Jesus. God gave Joseph instructions in 3 dreams to keep Jesus safe. Dream 1: "Danger! Escape to Egypt!" Dream 2: "All clear! Return to Israel." Dream 3: "Moving time. Take your family to Nazareth." Each time, Joseph obeyed God. Each time, God kept Joseph, Mary, and Jesus safe.

Squiggles feels startled at Joseph's strange dreams.

How does YOUR face look when you feel startled?

Cut out this prayer. Let family members take turns keeping it beside their bed at night. Say the prayer together at bedtime.

DEAR GOD, help us always to listen to you and obey you. Thank you for keeping us safe. Amen.

WHO KEEPS YOU SAFE? HOW? WHAT DO YOU LIKE ABOUT TRAVELING?

God kept Joseph, Mary, and Jesus safe on their long trip

How do the things or people in the pictures help to keep you safe? Talk about and practice the plan in your home to be safe in case of fire and bad weather.

Make Time for Computer Fun!

Use the Internet to find out more about Egypt. What did people eat in ancient Egypt? What do they eat today? Who were some famous pharaohs? How were the pyramids built? Chat about what kids must do to be safe when using the Internet. (Never give your name or contact information to unknown people; always ask permission before downloading anything, and so on.)

Do You Know? Answers: Abram and Sarai (Abraham and Sarah); Joseph; Moses; the Israelites

Do You Know?

Solve these riddles about Bible times people who either **visited** Egypt or **lived** in Egypt! God kept all these people safe!

1. We visited Egypt during a famine. But we are better known for God promising us a baby even though we were old.

We are _____.
(Genesis 12:10)

2. I wear a colorful coat and interpret dreams. My jealous brothers sold me into slavery and I was taken to Egypt.

I am _____.
(Genesis 37:25-28)

3. I was born in Egypt and adopted by a princess. As an adult, I asked the pharaoh to free my people.

I am _____.
(Exodus 2:1-10)

4. Baby Jesus escaped *to* Egypt. Many years earlier, we escaped *from* Egypt. We are Jesus' ancestors.

We are _____.
(Exodus 13:17-18)

In the Bible AND In Our World!

Egypt is a very old country in North Africa. Some things, such as camels and pyramids, look the same today as when Joseph and his family escaped to Egypt. But Joseph wouldn't recognize many other things in Egypt today. Most Egyptians live near the banks of the Nile River in modern cities with cars and skyscrapers.

Make Time for Traveling Fun!

Joseph's family took 3 trips. What might they have packed each time? Grab an empty backpack or suitcase. Call out a destination (camp, beach, city, etc.) and give family members 5 minutes to pack 5 items. Discuss whether these were really the best choices. Then repeat with another destination.

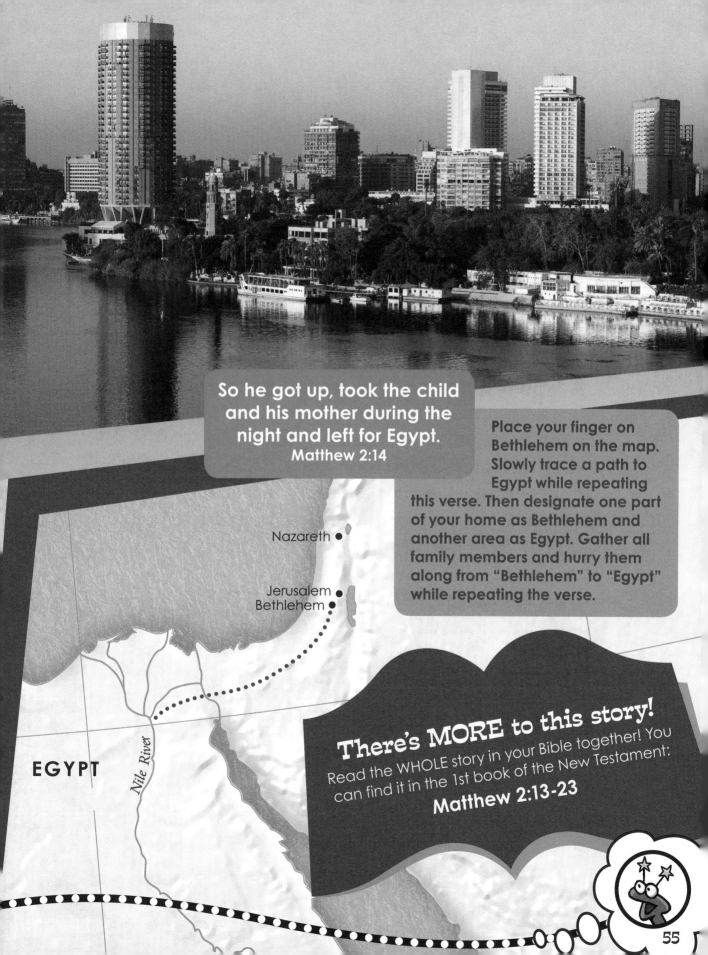

So he got up, took the child and his mother during the night and left for Egypt.
Matthew 2:14

Place your finger on Bethlehem on the map. Slowly trace a path to Egypt while repeating this verse. Then designate one part of your home as Bethlehem and another area as Egypt. Gather all family members and hurry them along from "Bethlehem" to "Egypt" while repeating the verse.

Nazareth ●

Jerusalem ●
Bethlehem ●

EGYPT

Nile River

There's MORE to this story!
Read the WHOLE story in your Bible together! You can find it in the 1st book of the New Testament:
Matthew 2:13-23

Simeon and Anna

God shows up!

When Mary and Joseph brought baby Jesus to the temple, they were in for a surprise. People were waiting for Jesus! God had promised a man named Simeon that he would live long enough to see the Messiah. When he saw Jesus, Simeon *knew* God had kept the promise! A prophet named Anna also recognized that Jesus was the Messiah God promised.

A prophet is a person God chooses to share God's messages with the world.

SURPRISE! SURPRISE! SURPRISE! SURPRISE! SURPRISE! SURPRISE! SURPRISE! SURPRISE! SURPRISE! SURPRISE! SURPRISE! SURPRISE! SURPRISE! SURPRISE! SURPRISE! SURPRISE! SURPRISE! SURPR

WHAT PROMISES TAKE A LONG TIME?

WHERE DO YOU SEE GOD IN YOUR LIFE?

Squiggles feels grateful. God kept God's promise!

How does **YOUR** face look when you feel grateful?

GOD, help us always look for you to show up in our lives! Amen.

Cut out this prayer and slip it into a family photo album. Pray it together whenever you look at the photos.

Bringing Jesus to the temple was an important event for his family.

Look at the photos. How does your family celebrate events like these?

Make Time for Family Photo Fun!

Spend time looking at baby pictures of people in your family. What similarities do you see? What differences?

SURPR SURPRISE! SURPRISE! SURPRISE! SURPRI

There's MORE to this story!

Read the WHOLE story in your Bible together!
You can find it in the 3rd book of the New Testament:

Luke 2:22-40

In the Spark Story Bible, look for the New Testament story titled *Simeon and Anna* on pages 210-213.

Draw a family celebration of your own.

The child grew and became strong; he was filled with wisdom, and the grace of God was on him.
Luke 2:40

Take turns reading this verse, but wait one minute in between each person reading. What is it like to have to wait to hear about Jesus?

ME

THANK YOU
VERY MUCH

Thank you

thank you

Make Time for Art Fun!

Simeon and Anna were both grateful to God for the arrival of Jesus! Pick a time when your family can make thank-you cards for each other. Start with blank paper to make unique creations that express why you are thankful for each other.

SURPRISE! SURPRISE! SURPR SURPRISE! SURPRISE! SURPR

What does this word mean to you?

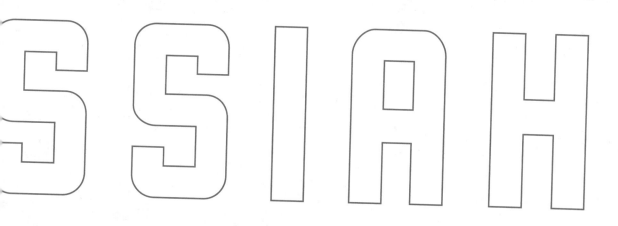

SSIAH

COLOR THIS WORD. *Messiah* means "the chosen one" in Hebrew. God promised to send a child who would save the world. That child was Jesus. Read the words of an angel of the Lord proclaiming the birth of Jesus, the Messiah, in Luke 2:8-12.

Do You Know?

Jesus was born in one town. He grew up in a different town. The temple for God was in a third city!

Do you know these three places? Fill in the vowels to spell out the names of these three towns. *(Hint: Find all of the answers in Luke 2.)*

A E I O U

Jesus was born in:

B___THL___H___M

Jesus grew up in:

N___Z___R___TH

The temple was in:

J___R___S___L___M

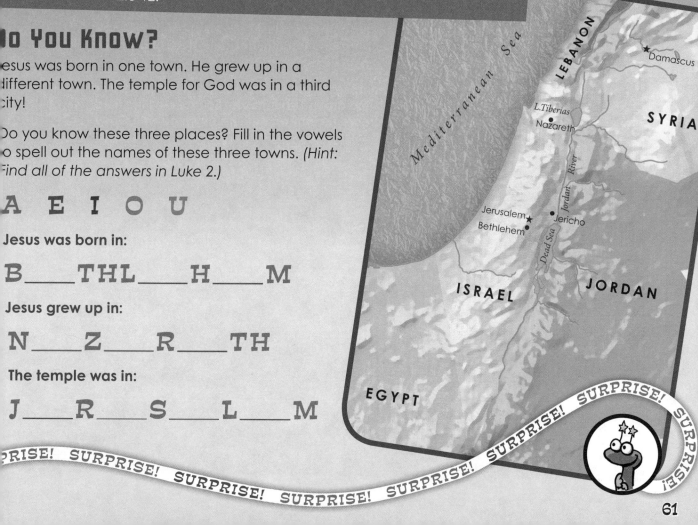

SURPRISE! SURPRISE! SURPRISE! SURPRISE! SURPRISE! SURPRISE! SURPRISE! SURPRISE! SURPRISE!

A Note for Grown-Ups

At Sparkhouse Family, we believe faith formation isn't something that only happens when kids are in church or hearing a Bible story in Sunday school. It's an ongoing process that's part of every moment of a child's life. Each interaction with a caring adult shows kids what love looks like. Each playful interaction with a friend taps into their God-given joy and delight. Moments of daydreaming and imaginative play develop their ability to see God in the world.

We also know that many families want to create intentional times of spiritual formation for their kids. That's where the Spark Story Bible Play and Learn books come in. Whether you've already introduced your children to the Bible or are just starting to talk about it, these books make a great resource for helping your family dive into God's Word. They offer a hands-on approach to teaching Bible stories that will resonate with your whole family. Together, you'll explore these stories through games, puzzles, conversation, prayer, and easy-to-manage activities. You can spend ten minutes on a story or a whole afternoon—it's all up to you.

And you won't need a long list of supplies to get started—some crayons, a pair of scissors, and a few items you can find around your house. So make a little time, grab a handful of crayons, and create fun, meaningful family time with God.

Thanks!

Sparkhouse Family

Image Credits

Image Credits (continued)